IT'S SPRING!

IT'S SPRING!

Text
and
Photographs
by
SISTER NOEMI WEYGANT, O.S.B.

THE WESTMINSTER PRESS
Philadelphia

STANDARD BOOK No. 664-32437-1

LIBRARY OF CONGRESS CATALOG CARD No. 69-12667

BOOK DESIGN BY
DOROTHY ALDEN SMITH

Published by The Westminster Press ®
Philadelphia, Pennsylvania

PRINTED IN THE UNITED STATES OF AMERICA

CONTENTS

THE SOUL OF SPRING

AT the recent National Convention of the Professional Photographers of America, in Chicago, Sister Noemi showed slides of her pictures and read poems that she had written for them. They covered the four seasons of the year. Many of them were from the spring series—the same pictures and poems that appear in this book. As she read, with the pictures on the screen, the very soul of spring seemed to come into the room. The spirit of everyone listening was refreshed and nurtured.

Through the years I have seen Sister Noemi develop her great talent to interpret and to give us the beauty and wonder of God's world through her camera's eye.

I treasure her honesty, her enthusiasm, her courage, her artistry, and her friendship.

Virginia Stern

SPRING IS . . .

Oh come,
  oh run
    to the woodlands with me.

Listen,
  see how everything,
  everywhere,
    is blooming,
    nesting,
    sprouting,
    growing,
    leafing,
    blowing,
    feathering,
    mating.

Spring is being new.

Spring is—I love you.

Spring is—love.

SPRING'S FIRST RAIN

Spring's first rain
   coming after months
   of snow
      is always—delight.

To everything
   it finds,
      rain gives light
      and design.
We marvel.

Then—THUNDER!
After long silence
   of winter
      thunder seems
      a nature wonder.

Each little drop
   is held like a jewel
   until a new one comes
      to roll it down
      into the ground.

Suddenly,
   winter is forgotten.

ONLY FOR THE HEART

An old fall feather,
   after a long winter,
      is a harp.

The sun,
   gliding through weeds
   where the harp hangs,
      runs light fingers
      over
      frail feather strings.

Spring breezes
   flow
   through the strings,
   beautifully,
      for a breeze
      is
      a skilled harpist.

Sun and breeze
   together
   create a melody,
      but only the heart is tuned
      to their song.
Listen carefully.

THEY CAN'T TAKE WING

Not all trees
   waken at the same time
      in spring.

It's not unusual,
   therefore,
      to find in a bleak forest,
   one tree
   with leaves
   arriving so rapidly
      they appear
      to be birds.

They can't take wing,
   but if you listen,
      you may hear them sing.

NO VISITORS, PLEASE

Hush!
No visitors, please.
The forest
   is a maternity floor.

This new flower,
   wrapped in a blanket,
   green-blue,
     needs a day or so
     for warming,
     growing.

When again
   you pass by,
   however,
     you'll discover
     the flower in full bloom.

It will be
   a white star,
   shining
   through the brown leaves,
     heralding spring
     with sphery song.

WHERE IS THE MOTHER?

A loon mother
   builds her nest
   over the water,
      because her feet
      were made for swimming.

I wonder—
   where is she now?

Has she gone
   for a swim?
Has she gone
   in search of food?

Has an enemy
   destroyed her,
      leaving the egg abandoned?

Though the sun
   is kind
   and warm,
      it will never hatch the egg.

Oh Mother Loon,
I know
   you won't return
      so long as I stand here.

I'll go.

But please
   come back
      before your egg gets cold!

A CHILD'S SPOON

This fuzzy
  forest child
  has
    a copper-plated spoon.

He should hurry
  and lick it dry,
    or the sun will.

But does it hold
  a drop of rain
  or dew?
Maybe
  that spoon holds
  a vitamin pill
    that Mother bought
    so her child would grow
    into a champion.

Now comes a question:

A champion what?

AM I HAVING SECRETS?

Some call me
   Showy Lady.

Am I having secrets
   with my dearest friend,
     or gazing
     at my own reflection
     in a water mirror?

Can you put your foot
   into my slipper
     and tie
     my ribbon laces
     with a bow?

I wonder
   if an Indian girl
     once wore me for dancing
     on moist moss
     in a shady bower . . .

DID SPRING MAKE A MISTAKE?

Oh!

This must be a mistake,
   for surely spring
   would not give
   such lovely wing
   to anything,
      then tie it to a tree . . .

These leaves
   were surely meant to be
   a butterfly,
      floating wide,
      and high.

Please
   cut me free?
If you do,
   I will take you along
      with me.

SO NEAR, SO FAR AWAY

I am a tiny black ant
  that, by mistake,
  climbed
  onto a snowball
    one bright day.

I did not know
  that spring
  had not yet
    melted its ice away.

Once started,
  there was nothing to do
  but keep crawling.

But now I am in great danger.
Out here where I am
  an enemy can
    so easily spot me!

SPRING CLOWNS

We are clowns
   dangling down
   like balloons
      on a slender stem.

Spring
   is bright
   and singy.

But
   when its moods
   turn cold,
   and blowy,
   and weepy,
   we're here
   to make spring laugh
      again.

WILL THEY FIT YOUR BABY?

Flower mittens,
   pearly-pink,
   knitted for the twins
   to wear
     till after the last chill
     of spring.

But then,
   the twins
     will soon outgrow them.

Do you know
   a little baby
   who could wear
     these flower mittens?

DON'T BETRAY ME!

See...
   a baby grasshopper
   gently cradled
   in sleep
     by a meadow breeze...

Bedded in pollen down
   with the sun to incubate him—
   won't be long
   before he grows
     into a grown-up grasshopper,
   unless
   a hungry bird
     finds him asleep,

Snap!

A GUESSING GAME

Am I climbing up
   or coasting down?
Is my pole
   a blade of grass
     or a weed?

Can you count
   the number of buttons
   on my black and gold,
   double-breasted
     caterpillar coat?

How many bracelets
   do I wear?

What do I eat
   while I'm a caterpillar?
What will my name be
   when
     I become a butterfly?

35

WHERE AM I?

Why are you staring at me so?

If you think I'm a strange creature,
   don't you know
   I may be thinking the same
     about you?

My eyes, like yours,
   are smaller than my ears.
Though man has had many kinds of glasses
   through the years,
   the gold-rimmed kind
   have always been in fashion
     in my frog family.

You realize, I'm sure,
   that all this time
     my big eye has been watching you . . .

Waiting!

It's a game frogs have been playing
   with children
     since time began.
Your big hand is coming near—nearer,
   closing like a cup
     to scoop me up.

Down! Splash! Jump! Alas!

I beat you to it.

Where am I?

OUR PUSSY WILLOW

Come, children,
   the silver pussy willow
   is blooming—
      first little creature
      of spring.

Rub the catkin
   against your cheek.
Is it furry?

Put it to your ear.
Is it purry?

HAPPY DANDELION

Oh golden, laughing dandelion,
  always playing
  with grasses
  that ripple
  and shine.

Your bloom brightens
  Mother's first bunch
    of spring flowers.

With your stems
  we make
    a long, gay chain.

When
  you're done with flowering,
    we blow you away.

Let Dad
  keep on digging and mowing.
Children love you
  for
    growing.

CHEWY LIKE GUM

The pine tree
  in spring,
    wears waxy earrings.

In the sun,
  they shine.
In the mouth,
  they are chewy
    like gum.

SPRING ARROWS

Spring grows
    its own
    bow
    and arrows.

Only
    the cattail reed
    could use
    such a weapon
    perfectly,
        because of
        its rare sensitivity.

However,
    if you wish,
    you may borrow
    the outfit
    long enough
        to shoot
        an arrow.

Just be careful
    how
        you choose your target.

AM I A HELMET?

Am I a helmet for you to wear
   when you race in your Honda?

Or am I a sort of balloon
   to ride you to the moon?

Will I stick you
   if you put a finger
   to one of my pins?

Try it!

April Fool!
I'm only a spongy mushroom.

WHERE?

Mrs. Chipmunk,
 alone,
 on a stone,
  why are you so fat?

I know,
I know,
 you're like my cat—
  you're going to have babies.

I wish,
 I wish
 that I knew where,
 for I would hold one—
  oh, so carefully.

VALUABLE ANTIQUE

The gas-burning lamp
  belongs
  to the long ago.

Hanging down
  from the ceiling,
    it looked like
    this twig.

When gas
  at the end
  of the tube
  was lit,
    there was light
    for nighttime.

Must be,
  the red maple tree,
  who burns
  such a lamp
  each spring,
    likes antique
    treasures.

MARSH MARIGOLD

It's spring, spring,
   my time for blooming.

I sing, sing,
   with the wild birds,
   and the songs
   of running water.

My name is—
   Marsh Marigold.

I grow
   in swampland,
   or along the banks
   of creeks
   and rivers.

I invite you
   to take home
     one of my new bouquets.

WATCH YOUR FEET!

Peek—peep!

No,
I'm not a little chick
   pecking through an eggshell.

I'm so very tiny,
   but I'm alive,
   and I'm afraid
     that you will step
     on me.

So peek—peep,
   watch your feet!

WE KEEP FAILING

We are shooting stars
    sent down to earth
        in the invasion
        of creation.

But, for some reason
    we cannot fathom,
        we have not yet made
        a landing.

If you are smart
    in school,
        maybe you can tell us
        why we never
        glide down
        to the ground.

THE THREE GUARDS

Orange rockets
   are shooting up
   from the ground
   through plant blades,
    to protect
    a little nest.

Is the life there
   bud or bird?

What does it matter?

Bird
   or bud,
     it's very precious.

MY NAME IS POLYPHEMUS

Hello!
I realize
I look like
  some garment
    tossed aside.

I'm wrinkly
  and dampish
  because
    I'm newly out of the cocoon
    where I spent winter.

I must say
  I'm surprised
  to discover
    that I'm no longer
    a caterpillar.

As soon as I'm dry
  and my wingspread free,
    I'll fly . . . fly . . . fly . . .
    into the evening.

There,
  another moth
    is waiting for me.

61

SIGN OF SUMMER

When first you see
    the small shadow
    of the empty stem
    of a violet,
    when you first find its petals,
    lying,
    drying,
        on its heart-shaped leaf . . .

Then you know
    spring
        is coming to an end.

Soon
    you'll meet summer,
    just around
    the bend,
        or down
        another street.